PIANO/VOCAL/CHORDS

# THE Best IN CHRISTMAS SHEET MUSIC

# CONTENTS

All I Want For Christmas Is My Two Front Teeth ...20

Deck The Halls ...................................... 6

Gesu Bambino .....................................14

The Gift ...............................................38

God Rest Ye Merry, Gentlemen .........................22

Hark! The Herald Angels Sing ........................ 8

Have Yourself A Merry Little Christmas ...............24

A Holly Jolly Christmas................................26

It's The Most Wonderful Time Of The Year ..........3

Jingle Bells............................................32

Jolly Old Saint Nicholas................................34

Let It Snow! Let It Snow! Let It Snow! .................36

The Little Drummer Boy .................................44

Merry Christmas, Darling................................11

The Most Wonderful Day Of The Year .................48

O Come, All Ye Faithful (Adeste Fideles)..............43

O Come, O Come, Emmanuel .........................50

Rockin' Around The Christmas Tree....................64

Rudolph, The Red-Nosed Reindeer .....................28

Santa Claus Is Comin' To Town .........................58

Silent Night .............................................52

Sleigh Ride ...........................................55

The Twelve Days Of Christmas.........................66

We Three Kings Of Orient Are .........................31

We Wish You A Merry Christmas .......................60

Winter Wonderland ....................................62

# IT'S THE MOST WONDERFUL
# TIME OF THE YEAR

By EDDIE POLA
and GEORGE WYLE

It's the Most Wonderful Time of the Year - 3 - 1

4

# DECK THE HALLS

Traditional

# HARK! THE HERALD ANGELS SING

Words and Music by
FELIX MENDELSSOHN
and CHAS. WESLEY

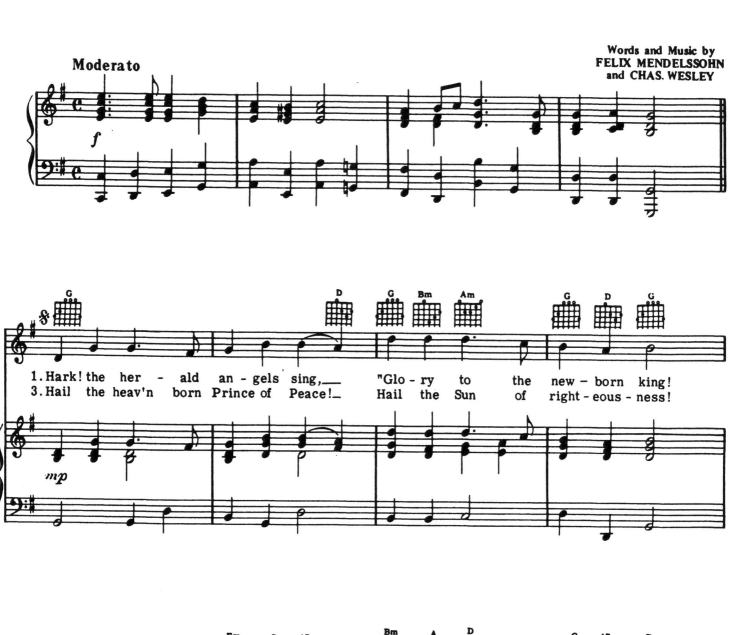

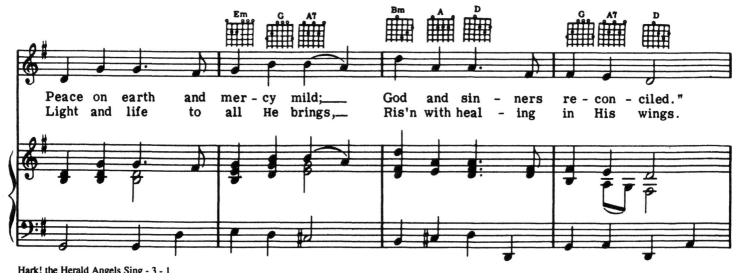

Hark! the Herald Angels Sing - 3 - 1

# MERRY CHRISTMAS, DARLING

Lyric by FRANK POOLER

Music by RICHARD CARPENTER

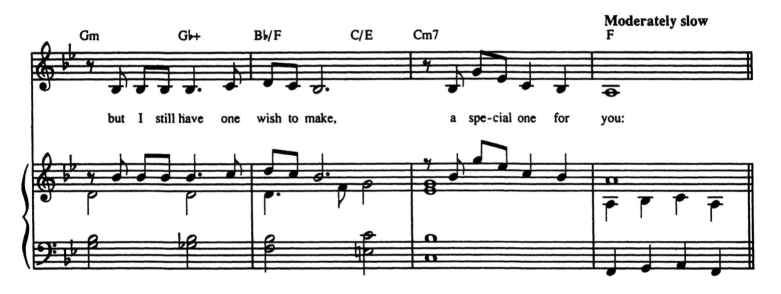

Merry Christmas, Darling - 3 - 1

12

# GESÙ BAMBINO
### (The Infant Jesus)

Words by
**FREDERICK H. MARTENS**
Italian Version by
**PIETRO A. YON**

Music by
**PIETRO A. YON**

**Andante mosso**

When

blos - soms flow - ered 'mid the snows Up - on a win - ter night Was

born the Child, the Christ - mas Rose, The King of Love and Light. The

\* In bars 3-6 and where passage is repeated the melody in the accompaniment may be played on chimes. The introduction may be treated in like manner.

Gesù Bambino - 6 - 1

an - gels sang, the shep-herds sang, The grate - ful earth re - joiced,

And at His bless - ed birth the stars Their ex - ul - ta - tion

voiced. O come let us a -

**Non troppo lento**

*sentito*

dore Him, O come let us a - dore Him, O

come let us a - dore ____ Him, Christ ____ the

Lord. _____ A -

**Tempo I**

gain __ the heart __ with rap - ture glows To greet the ho - ly night ____ That

# ALL I WANT FOR CHRISTMAS IS MY TWO FRONT TEETH

Words and Music by
DON GARDNER

All I Want for Christmas Is My Two Front Teeth - 2 - 1

# GOD REST YE MERRY, GENTLEMEN

TRADITIONAL

God Rest Ye Merry Gendemen - 2 - 1

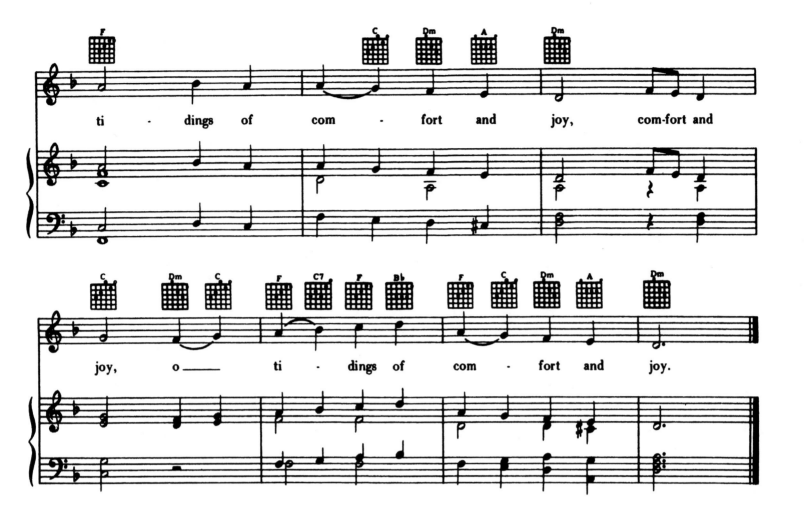

3. In Bethlehem, in Jewry
This blessed Babe was born,
And laid within a manger
Upon this holy morn,
The which his Mother Mary
Did nothing take in scorn.
O tidings, etc.

4. "Fear not then," said the Angel,
"Let nothing you affright,
This day is born a Saviour
Of a pure Virgin bright,
To free all those who trust in Him
From Satan's power and might."
O tidings, etc.

5. The shepherds at those tidings
Rejoiced much in mind,
And left their flocks a-feeding,
In tempest, storm, and wind:
And went to Bethlehem straightway,
The Song of God to find.
O tidings, etc.

6. And when they came to Bethlehem
Where our dear Saviour lay,
They found Him in a manger,
Where oxen feed on hay;
His Mother Mary kneeling down,
Unto the Lord did pray.
O tidings, etc.

7. Now to the Lord sing praises,
All you within this place,
And with true love and brotherhood
Each other now embrace;
This holy tide of Christmas
All other doth deface.
O tidings, etc.

# HAVE YOURSELF
# A MERRY LITTLE CHRISTMAS

Words and Music by
HUGH MARTIN and
RALPH BLANE

Have Yourself A Merry Little Christmas - 2 - 1

Have Yourself A Merry Little Christmas - 2 - 2

*From the Videocraft T.V. Musical Spectacular "RUDOLPH THE RED-NOSED REINDEER"*

# A HOLLY JOLLY CHRISTMAS

By JOHNNY MARKS

A Holly Jolly Christmas - 2 - 1

# RUDOLPH, THE RED-NOSED REINDEER

Words and Music by
JOHNNY MARKS

Rudolph, the Red-Nosed Reindeer - 3 - 1

# WE THREE KINGS OF ORIENT ARE

JOHN H. HOPKINS

# JINGLE BELLS

J. PIERPONT

Jingle Bells - 2 - 1

*Chorus:*

sleigh - ing song to - night! Jin - gle bells, jin - gle bells, jin - gle all the

way, Oh, what fun it is to ride in a one - horse o - pen

sleigh!___ Jin - gle bells, jin - gle bells, jin - gle all the way,

Oh, what fun it is to ride in a one - horse o - pen sleigh!

# JOLLY OLD ST. NICHOLAS

TRADITIONAL

Jolly Old St. Nicholas - 2 - 1

Jolly Old St. Nicholas - 2 - 2

# LET IT SNOW! LET IT SNOW! LET IT SNOW!

Lyric by
SAMMY CAHN

Music by
JULE STYNE

Let It Snow! Let It Snow! Let It Snow! - 2 - 1

# THE GIFT

Words and Music by
JIM BRICKMAN and
TOM DOUGLAS

**Slowly** ♩ = 72

*(with pedal)*

*Verse 1:*

*She:*

1. Win-ter snow is fall-ing___ down, chil-dren laugh-ing all a - round.

Lights are turn-ing on, like a fair-y tale___ come true.___ Sit-tin' by the fire we___ made.

The Gift - 5 - 1

The Gift - 5 - 2

*Verse 2:*

2. Watch-ing as you soft - ly___ sleep. What I'd give if I___ could___ keep just this mo-ment. If

on - ly time___ stood still. But the col - ors fade_____ a-way and the years will make us___ gray.___

___ But, ba-by, in my eyes,___ you'll still be beau-ti - ful._____ And all I want___

# O COME, ALL YE FAITHFUL
## (ADESTE FIDELES)

JOHN READING

2. Sing, choirs of angels,
Sing in exultation,
Sing, all ye citizens of heaven above:
Glory to God
In the highest glory!
O come, let us adore Him, etc.

3. Yea, Lord, we greet Thee,
Born this happy morning,
Jesus, to Thee be glory giv'n,
Word of the Father,
Now in flesh appearing.
O come, let us adore Him, etc.

# THE LITTLE DRUMMER BOY

Words and Music by
KATHERINE DAVIS,
HENRY ONORATI
and HARRY SIMEONE

The Little Drummer Boy - 4 - 1

The Little Drummer Boy - 4 - 3

I played my best for Him, pa - rum pum pum pum, rum pum pum pum,

rum pum pum pum.____

Then He smiled at me pa - rum pum pum pum,____

me and my drum.____

The Little Drummer Boy - 4 - 4

# THE MOST WONDERFUL DAY OF THE YEAR

Words and Music by
JOHNNY MARKS

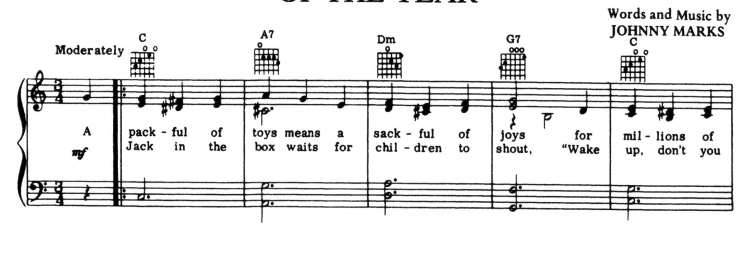

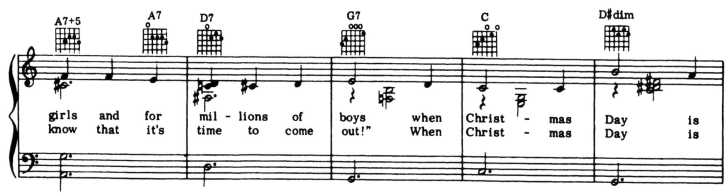

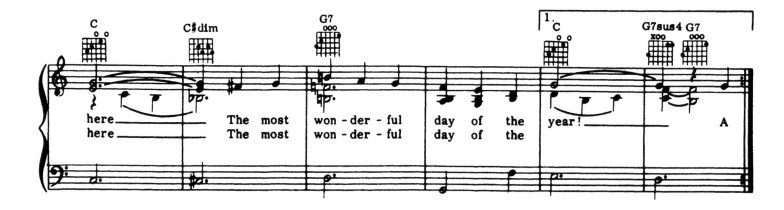

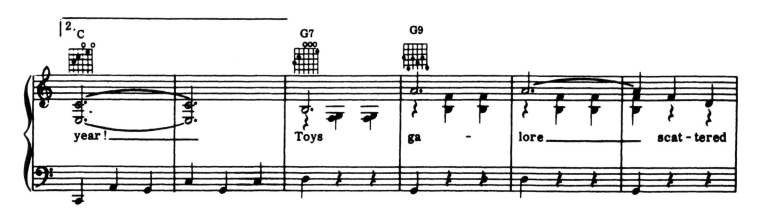

The Most Wonderful Day Of The Year - 2 - 1

# O COME, O COME EMMANUEL

English lyric by
JOHN M. NEALE
Moderately

Music adapted by
THOMAS HELMORE

O Come, O Come Emmanuel - 2 - 1

3. O come, Thou Day-Spring, come and cheer
   Our spirits by Thine advent here;
   Disperse the gloomy clouds of night,
   And Death's dark shadows put to flight.
   *Chorus*

4. O come, Thou Key of David, come,
   And open wide our heav'nly home;
   Make safe the way that leads on high,
   And close the path to misery.
   *Chorus*

5. O come, O come, Thou Lord of might,
   Who to Thy tribes, on Sinai's height,
   In ancient times did'st give the law,
   In cloud, and majesty and awe.
   *Chorus*

# SILENT NIGHT

Words and Music by
**JOSEPH MOHR** and
**FRANZ GRUBER**

Silent Night - 3 - 1

Silent Night - 3 - 2

# SLEIGH RIDE

Words by
MITCHELL PARISH

Music by
LEROY ANDERSON

**Moderately bright**

Just hear those sleigh bells jin-gle-ing, ring-ting-tin-gle-ing, too, ____

____ Come on, it's love-ly weath-er for a Sleigh Ride to-geth-er with you, ____

____ Out-side the snow is fall-ing and friends are call-ing "Yoo hoo,"

Sleigh Ride - 3 - 1

# SANTA CLAUS IS COMIN' TO TOWN

Words by
**HAVEN GILLESPIE**

Music by
**J. FRED COOTS**

Moderately

You bet-ter watch out, you bet-ter not cry, Bet-ter not pout, I'm

tell-ing you why: San-ta Claus is com-in' to town.

He's mak-ing a list and check-ing it twice, Gon-na find out who's

naught-y and nice, San-ta Claus is com-in' to town.

Santa Claus Is Coming To Town - 2 - 1

# WE WISH YOU A MERRY CHRISTMAS

TRADITIONAL ENGLISH CAROL

We Wish You A Merry Christmas - 2 - 1

# WINTER WONDERLAND

Words by
DICK SMITH

Music by
FELIX BERNARD

Winter Wonderland - 2 - 1

# ROCKIN' AROUND THE CHRISTMAS TREE

By JOHNNY MARKS

Rockin' Around - 2 - 1

# THE TWELVE DAYS OF CHRISTMAS

TRADITIONAL

The Twelve Days Of Christmas - 3 - 1